Market Your Sizzle Using a Big Outrageous Shocking Positive Wow

ISBN: 978-1-312-83384-5

Product ID: 16192981

Category: Business & Economics

Copyright: Standard Copyright License

Author: Bob Oros

Edition: First

Published: September 16, 2019

Description: Are you a web designer, online marketer, small business owner, or entrepreneur having a hard time selling your products and services? Have you ever sent an email thinking you had a great pitch only to have it fall flat with zero response? Have you created a sales letter, postcard, flyer or brochure only to have it end up in the trash? The design and graphics are important to create a successful campaign, however, it's the COPY that makes the sale. If you design a great looking website the compelling copy will get visitors to click the buy button. If you are sending an email, it's the persuasive copy that gets the response. If you are writing a flyer or brochure it's the words you use that will get them to pick it up. If you are sending a postcard, the powerful words you use will get them to act. Once you see how easy it is to write compelling sales copy you will not only increase your own sales, you will be able to really help your customers with more sales and more commissions for you.

Key words: market your sizzle, wow marketing, marketing ideas, writing headlines, sales letter copy, copy writing techniques.

Contents

Are you having a hard time selling your products and services?

What is the solution? It is NOT "waiting for a customer to contact me." If that is your approach, it will never happen! It's learning how to approach your customer with a NEW, UP TO DATE selling and marketing strategy.

What is the new strategy? It is so simple that once you discover it and begin to use it you will be amazed at your results! Knowing this strategy will change the way you look at EVERY business, EVERY billboard, EVERY television and radio advertisement, EVERY menu, EVERY marketing piece, EVERY sales presentation, EVERYTHING YOU BUY OR SELL!

- Scott Nachatilo, a highly successful real estate investor and trainer, increased his response rate from zero to FORTY FIVE PERCENT by simply including this in his offer!

- A company in the Midwest used this strategy and within a few months went from a negative growth right back up to a 27% sales increase.

- I recently discussed this with a group of 60 restaurant

owners and EVERY ONE of them agreed whole heartedly that this was the MAGIC KEY for appealing to today's new customer.

- An audience of more than 200 assisted living administrators said this was the most encouraging information they have heard in YEARS! They now know the enemy. They know what weapon to use to win the battle!

- Once you know what it is and start to identify it IN YOUR OWN BUSINESS, you will say "of course, why didn't I see that before?"

Once you know what it is you will not only know the key to increasing your own sales, you will be able to really help your customers get back on track with more sales and more profits.

I have built this MAGIC KEY into all my sales training seminars and the results are amazing. I have made this principle the premise for all my association presentations, Chamber of Commerce meetings, special event keynotes and food show seminars and the audience is immediately MOTIVATED to go back to their business and attack their operation with a whole new mindset. I have implemented this with dozens of small companies, and they have kissed the self-inflicted recession goodbye!

I am going to let you in on a little secret. I know this secret because I travel all over the country and talk with salespeople, business owners and entrepreneurs face to face, one-to-one.

Here's the secret: Business as we have known it is never going to be the same. There is a big shakedown in the works and thousands of companies are going to go by the wayside. They are run by people who just don't get it.

As they go out of business there is going to be an amazing surge of sales for those people who have made the transition. For those people who are willing to act NOW and not sit and wait until "customers beat a pathway to my door!" Face it. It is NEVER going to happen. This is the new economy!

Here Is the Magic Key.

As we said, people are more savvy, conservative and thrifty than ever before. We HAVE to offer them something BOLD AND SHOCKING or we will just be another "me too" that will soon fade away.

Let me give you an example. I recently had a house for sale. It was rented for the previous three years and the tenants didn't take very good care of the place. The rugs were ruined, the walls were dirty, the whole place looked shabby.

I wanted to get rid of it, so I offered it for sale "as is" for a fairly low price. As I was cleaning the place up several prospects walked through the house with little interest. There was not one offer. No one was interested.

That house in that condition reminds me of dozens of businesses I know of. They are simply there with nothing to offer, nothing exciting, and nothing interesting.

Here is what the house needed. It needed a WOW! It needed something that caught the attention of the prospect and made them say a POSITIVE, SINCERE WOW!

I went to work and took out all the carpets, completely painted the inside of the house and then went to work on not one, not two, but 5 WOWS!

WOW # 1. Fireplace.

As soon as you walked in the front door the first thing you see is a huge brick fireplace. I painted the entire brick surface with polyurethane. The entire wall was brick and it looked so good it would practically jump out and scream "look at me – I am beautiful!"

WOW # 2. The kitchen cabinets.

Scratches and faded stain made the kitchen cabinets look old and worn out. I purchased some "restore" and like magic, they came to life. They were so stunning that they created a second "wow!"

WOW # 3. Sunroom.

Just off the living room was a sunroom that looked nice, but it was not anything special. I went to the flooring store and purchased some oak laminated floor. This COMPLETELY changed the room to third "wow!"

WOW # 4. The outside deck.

The house has a HUGE deck with a great place for a swimming pool. The deck was faded and didn't have a lot of appeal. A fresh coat of stain and presto! This was the fourth wow!

WOW # 5. The office.

One of the bedrooms was converted into an office. It has some great oak cabinets, tile floor, a super bookcase and a door that went out to the deck. A little more "restore" on the wood, some polish on the floor and a flyer that showed how easily this could be converted back into a great bedroom and the final wow was created.

Once the carpets were installed THE FIRST PERSON WHO WALKED THROUGH THE HOUSE BOUGHT IT!

Why? Because that is what it takes to sell to today's new consumer.

Now let's take a ride down highway 635 in Dallas.

I was on my way to talk to a group of 60 restaurant owners. I wanted to give them current PROOF of how the POSITIVE WOW is making a difference in the business of several chain restaurants. Here is what I saw on the 30-mile stretch:

Outback Steak House: for years it has always been fairly expensive to eat a steak at the Outback. They now have a complete steak dinner for $9.99. That qualifies as a WOW!

Denny's: in addition to the new menu items they have, which gives you a choice of several ways to build the Grand Slam, they had a FREE breakfast a while ago. Thousands of people took advantage of it. A FREE breakfast qualifies as a WOW!

Olive Garden: the marketing of their new menu items at lower prices, along with their theme "when you're here, your family" qualifies as a WOW!

Luby's Café: there were not one, but two billboards with great pictures of their meal deal for $5.99. Two in 30 miles… that's gets a wow!

Hotel $25 per night: OK, that's not a food wow, but, nevertheless, $25 for a hotel room get's a wow as long as you can sleep in it!

Quiznos: They have come out with their new "torpedo" sandwich line. Less than $5.00 and they have a buy one, get one for a penny! TWO sandwiches for less than $5.00. WOW!

IHOP: There new marketing campaigns of menu items. They are GREAT. Big enough to split between two people. They definitely get a WOW!

What-A-Burger: They are a regional chain, but with their new marketing campaign they really make the burgers and sandwiches look good. Their prices are very competitive and the combination get's a WOW!

Braums: They are also a regional chain and have always had a WOW with their advertisement of a banana split. Looks so good you don't even have to be hungry to eat one. WOW, it really looks good!

Pizza Hut: Always coming up with something new. The

"ring of cheese" and the guy saying "JACKPOT" on the commercial get's the job done. Also, their new line of pasta. I don't know if it will make it, but it sure gets a WOW!

How many restaurants did I pass on the 30 mile stretch that simply said: "here I am, I am a restaurant?" The response to this is…. So what!

I think you get the point. Now, lets look at YOUR WOW. Do you have one? When you call on an account do you have something that will make your prospect say WOW? If not, you simply won't get the sale.

Let's look at your business. Like the house we talked about does your business have at least 3 or 4 WOW STATEMENTS that will grab your customer? If not, your customer will simply go somewhere else.

Figure out what you have to do to make your prospects and customers say WOW in a positive response to your product and service and you will be a winner.

There is too much "ho hum" marketing, selling and copywriting left over from when consumers were on the wave of spending and having everything they want. Today, people are different. Your sales and marketing must have a WOW! The more the better!

Read this book with the goal in mind of creating your WOW x 5!

WOW # 1 _____

WOW # 2 _____

WOW # 3 _____

WOW # 4 _____

WOW # 5 _____

Copywriting is the most important skill.

It is also an excellent way to drive customers to your web site to buy your products and services.

Nearly everyone in business will benefit by having a thorough understanding of how to write sales copy. No matter what product or service you are selling and marketing you will be able to increase your sales with copywriting savvy.

When I began selling sales training seminar's to large distribution companies, I packaged my program as a "direct mail product", built a mailing list and began marketing.

When I "got an order" I traveled to their company or convention, delivered my "product", picked up my check, and returned home. In a very short period of time my seminar fees exceeded one million dollars! While many people in the seminar business spend grueling hours on the telephone, I made nearly all of my sales with one or two phone calls.

I have also built a very comfortable business publishing manuals and providing consulting services in addition to my seminars. _All possible because 25 years ago I educated myself on selling via the post office._

When I first started my business career, I was part owner and manager of a meat company and was able to sell enough to keep 25 employees on the payroll, **mostly because of my direct marketing efforts**. Located in a remote part of the country that was mostly dependent on tourist business, I was able to sell many other products such as hams, bacon, and deerskin products during the off season via the mail.

During the 25 years that followed I can attribute many of my successes to the ability to write sales letters and marketing brochures and understanding the numbers and percentages involved.

There is only one sure way to learn the secrets of marketing savvy

1. Go to the post office and buy at least **30 stamped post cards**. Go to the news stand, pick up a dozen magazines, answer every ad offering "Free Details". Don't discriminate. Send for everything.

2. Go to the office supply store and buy **twelve small cardboard file boxes**. One for each month. Take the first box and mark it for the current month.

As all your "junk mail" and legitimate direct mail offers come, *read each one carefully and note which ones catch your attention and why.* Staple the marketing piece together including the envelope and put it in the box. At the end of the month bring out a new box and label it for the new month. After you do this for 12 months take the first box you started with, go through it, keep only the marketing material that you like and pitch the rest of it. Use that file box again for the month adding all your mail you receive. _This will not only be an education you cannot get anywhere at any price; it will become a valuable resource and reference when you write your own marketing material._ Some of my boxes have advertising that I have kept and referred to for over 20 years!

Learning the direct mail business is the boot camp of all selling and marketing

WOW! Copywriting

A One Word Movie Title Will Sell
For as Much as One Million Dollars

Copywriting, whether for a display ad, a classified ad, a sales letter or a brochure, is a learned skill. It is one that anyone can master with *study, practice, and perhaps some professional guidance.*

The first step is to realize that you are <u>writing to sell</u>. **Don't waste a word** - in today's visual world, people are much less accustomed to reading than they were a few years ago. So, when they read anything about your product or service, be sure that they get the message you want them to get. <u>*Don't think that just because you are writing a few paragraphs for a brochure that the rules of sound selling don't apply.*</u> Don't think that just because your product is bought and used by intelligent, sophisticated people that a sales pitch will repel them.

You, the consultant or business owner, want the prospect (the person you are targeting your writing towards) to do one of the following:

a) Immediately write a check or go to your website and order the book, product or service being advertised.

17

b) Call or email for further information.

Any sales letter that causes the reader to only pause in his or her thinking, to just admire the product, or to simply believe what's written about the product - **is not doing its job completely.**

The "copywriter" must know **exactly** what he or she wants the reader to do, and any sales letter that does not elicit the desired action is an <u>absolute waste of time and money</u>.

Never forget the basic rule of copywriting. If the sales letter is not read, it won't stimulate any sales.

YOUR HEADLINE, or lead sentence when no headline is used, has to make it more difficult for your prospect to ignore or pass over, than to stop and read your letter.

If you don't capture the **attention** of your reader with your headline, anything beyond is a **useless** effort and wasted money.

The **best headlines** are those that challenge the reader; that **involves his or her self-esteem**, and do not allow the reader to dismiss your question or claim with a simple yes or no. The idea is to **shock or shake** the reader out of his or her reverie and cause them to take notice of your attention getting statement.

Whenever, and as often as you can possibly work it in, you should use the word "**YOU**" in your headline, and throughout your copy. Your sales letter should be directed to "**ONE**" person, and the person reading your sales letter wants to feel that you're talking to him or her personally, *not everyone who lives on their street.*

Headlines

The **eye-catching** appeal of your ad must start with the headline.

Use the headline to *very quickly create a picture in the minds of the reader* - a **vision of all their problems** being solved, and attainment of the kind of solution they seek.

If your headline fails to catch the **attention** of your prospect, you cannot hope to capture him with the remainder of the ad, *because it will go unread!*

So, in writing your sales copy, put yourself in the shoes of your reader.

You have his attention for just a little while, so you must quickly interest him in your offer, show him how he can get what he wants, and then cause him to send immediately for your "solution" to his or her problems.

Your copy must exude **enthusiasm**, **excitement**, and a **positive attitude.** Don't be afraid to use a hard-sell approach!

Say what you feel and believe about your offer.

And use common, "everyday," but correct English.

It's the job of the headline to attract attention to the ad and get him or her into the copy.

Most beginners try to be *all things to all people* when they write headlines. It doesn't work.

These types of headlines must be general, and generalities will attract few readers.

The best headlines *single out the readers* you want to reach.

Not every reader of every magazine, newspaper, or website you advertise in or everyone who looks at a copy of your brochure or sales letter will be a prospect.

You're always better off striving to reach only those who represent the best potential customer.

How to attract the readers who count.

It's no trick to get people to respond to an offer for a free catalog.

But it's another thing to get a _good response from people who are real prospects and who are genuinely interested in your product._

To ensure that you get more of the latter, you should give a lot of thought to your advertising headlines.

If you refer to a need or a problem that your prospects have, you will have narrowed down the range of respondents to those who should have more than a passing interest. And, of course, when a benefit is apparent, you will hear from the best prospects.

A headline will encourage prospects to read the copy when it promises that the product will fill the need or solve a problem. Often the promise is in a subheading; trying to get everything into a single headline can result in too many words.

How to use different types of headlines.

The how-to headline

People are looking for answers. When your headline promises to tell them how to solve a problem they are having, you will have captured a reader. Be sure your copy fulfills the promise, even if the final answer doesn't lie in your copy but in a catalog, you will send if the reader requests it, you have fulfilled the promise in the headline.

The news headlines

New and now are words that are so overworked that most readers discount them almost immediately.

However, all readers are seeking something new and they want what they want now.

Your product may be new, but anything you can do to get rid of the overworked word "new" will help make your news headlines draw more readers. The solution to boring advertising is to make news instead of filling space.

News is almost never boring.

Make news, not jokes.

Jokes in ads are almost never funny.

News is a benefit.

The news that can honestly tell your potential buyer what he wants to hear.

Specifically, that your product or service is available, ready now, cheaper, more prestigious, an item they couldn't get until now, a lesson capable of learning or profiting from, something enhancing.

There are thousands of newsworthy benefits capable of attracting buyers, believers, boat-owners and even meat eaters.

The woods are full of customers united in the desire to be helped in some way: by a savings of time, money and steps, by advice on how to catch a fish, how to understand the meaning of life and the reality of death, how to live with calamity when they're chin deep in it.

You can do a lot of newsworthy "Marketing" things with just about any product.

For example, securities when they're approached as action items instead of problems: splits, reverse splits, buy backs, options-always, of course within the limits of prudence and law.

You can sell bonds, subordinated debentures, real estate, receivables, leases and make news at the same time; how pro or con the news is will depend on your use of PR.

If you don't understand the technique of getting news and other benefits into your marketing program-and how and why to tell her "what's in it for her"-your ads probably will reveal one or more of these easily avoided characteristics:

The message is unclear due to humor, art or copy clarity.

The message is unclear due to too many specifications and too few benefits.

If your promotional package lacks the news value, the magnetism of built-in benefits, as much as 90% of its cost is a gift to the media.

Don't place any advertising lacking consumer news value or benefits.

When the well is dry, seek out and discuss benefits offered by the competition.

The picture headlines

A strong visual can often be used to tell the story, and all the headline is expected to do is provide the transition to the copy.

The headline may just state what is seen in the picture-in terms of benefits-or it can be used to begin the copy.

Don't worry about redundancy in advertising.

Tell em' what you're going to tell 'em, tell 'em, and tell 'em what you told 'em.

The prediction headlines

When you use this approach, you will find it most effective to use the second person.

That is, use "you."

This headline makes a positive prediction and includes a very strong benefit.

'You will save over 50% with our system'.

The command headlines

When you can use a commanding statement that is in the reader's best interest, you will have a strong headline.

In a sense, the command headline is the prediction headline without the "you."

To be most effective, command headlines should be relatively short.

Consider this example: 'Cut your processing time in half with our system'.

This approach will work, but your copy should follow the style of the headline.

If you use the prediction approach, continue to talk in terms of what will happen when the product is used.

The command approach lends itself more to direct copy and a closing that suggests immediate further investigation by the reader.

The testimonial headline

Most people like to know how others have fared with the product being advertised, and a testimonial can be a productive way of answering the question and getting the copy read.

Be careful that you quote someone who will be respected by the readers.

The person may not be well known, but as long as he or she has a position that will be respected, you will be on safe ground. Make sure that the quote sounds natural.

If the person being quoted says something out of character (the quote was obviously created by the copywriter), you will have a very weak ad.

Of course, the testimonial doesn't necessarily have to be the words of an individual.

If you get permission from a user to say that the company increased production by 60 percent when your product was used, you will have a strong testimonial.

The short story headlines

The short story headline must lead into a short story or a brief piece of copy that gets the message across in story form.

Although the story approach often features people, it is not necessarily used to give testimonials.

More often than not, this approach is best used with a human-interest angle.

For example, a tax consultant could use something like this: 'Joe Young saved six thousand dollars on his taxes'.

Long copy is read and acted on.

Most people who tell you that people won't read long copy are responding defensively because they never read anything longer than the listings in TV Guide.

Don't listen to them.

Every publisher and every independent readership service say that long as well as short copy is read and acted on.

It's not the length that makes the difference, it's what's in it for the reader and how interesting it is.

Ten words in the hands of someone not interested can be tedious, but 1,000 words in the hands of a potential customer who has an interest in your product or service can be a joy to read.

However, there is one caution you should observe.

If your copy is going to be long, make sure that there is enough space to use a legible typeface.

If you're good, but long, copy is going to be set solid in seven-point type, it just won't do the job.

As a rule of thumb, try not to use text type any smaller than nine points.

Are you a "headline reader?"

If not, it might be a good hobby. Pick up the newspaper or a magazine and pay close attention to the headlines. **Which ones grab you and make you want to continue reading?** Which ones do you pass over and why? Do you know that the folks in Hollywood will pay as much as one million dollars for a one-word title if they think it is the right one? That proves the value of the headlines we use to sell our products and services.

Following are some of my headlines. Why do you think they are successful?

Headlines that sold over 2 million in speaking fees

With the Same Formulaic Certainty As A McDonalds Franchise, We Can Launch Your "2nd Career" In The Exciting, Prestigious Business Of Paid Professional Speaking.... We'll Show You How You Can Make 'at least' $5,000 - $10,000 for a 60- 90 Minute Speech... Even if the Last Time You Got up to Speak was in Mrs. Patterson's 3rd Grade Class

37 inside secrets the six million-dollar producers use to reach their sales and gross profit objectives

DO YOU KNOW THAT YOU WILL LOSE 25% OF YOUR CUSTOMERS THIS YEAR? HERE'S WHY

I just ate lunch at Vito's Ristorante... and it was great... I expected the Godfather to walk out of the kitchen at any minute... it was my first time there and I will return. Here's the point. You never know where your next great sales idea will come from... Well, I found it in the restroom at Vito's.

What if you had a sales rep selling six million dollars a year with a margin of 26%? That is a staggering gross profit of $1,560,000!

Here are some amazing test results that can drastically affect your bottom line.

The secret of a huge sales increase by a UNIPRO Distributor in Bangor Maine

IT IS IMPOSSIBLE FOR A SALES TRAINER TO DESCRIBE A PLACE THEY HAVE NEVER BEEN

Can a 4-hour seminar really increase your street sales, gross profit, account penetration as well as show you a more effective way to open new accounts? The answer to this question is yes, as long as:

Sorry you couldn't make it to the Pompano Beach sales meeting... It was a great success! With all the positive feedback from the salespeople they will certainly see a steady increase in their sales and gross profit... How about letting me show you what they learned?

Here's what Roger Skillman, Director of Marketing, said immediately following the More Gross Profit Seminar...

Catapult your business and career to the highest level of success with these two industry specific seminars that are not available from any other source at any price

$8,800 - That's how much Mike Alph received by mailing a one-page letter to his key vendors even though he already has an annual marketing program with all of them!

If you make a small investment in the MoreGrossProfit sales program and each one of your salespeople commit to 10 minutes a day for 90 days applying the discoveries that took me 35 years to learn, your sales and gross profit will SKYROCKET!

For many years I have been watching the evolution of the distribution business. Based on my personal observations – and my mailing list – there are many companies who are no longer with us. I am sure you can name one that used to be in your marketing area. Why? Mostly because of these 7 fatal mistakes.

Is Your Business Going To The Dogs - I hope so! It is hard to believe, but there are over 50 million hot dogs eaten every day in the United States. Let me show you how to take a bite out of that business

How To Make More Money Without Doing Any More Work

How to Save At Least $25,000 On Your Next New Sales Rep

It costs the federal government more than one million dollars a day to employ nearly 10,000 USDA meat and poultry inspectors who are physically present in every packing plant during every minute of operation. Here is what this means to YOU

Let's Cut Sales And Raise Expenses! That kind of talk wouldn't be too popular at the next board meeting, however, in real life it seems to be happening more and more. Here's what I mean

If Your Salespeople Could Do These Seven Things, How Much Would It Do For Your Street Business?

How to Motivate Everyone To Implement Everything They Learn At Your Next Conference or Company Meeting

Why eighty percent of all customers have the same complaint about the salespeople that call on them

Why only one in four salespeople close after a sales presentation

Why most sales presentations are based on the wrong thing

– trying to find needs

Why over half of all sales are made after five objections – most give up after one

Why over 90% of all sales are lost during the first minute of the presentation

Why nearly 80% of everyone who fails in sales fail for the same reason

How to Add $44,272 to Every Customer's Bottom Line Starting Immediately

It took almost two years for Eric Freeman, VP Sales USF Boston, to decide to have the More Gross Profit Seminar presented to his sales team. His comment... "I should have done this two years ago!"

My wife Jane asked me to write a letter to you because I am guilty... "You are only selling the program that you like to do." She said. "The More Gross Profit seminar is really good and will increase sales and profits, but it's not the one that gives the biggest benefit to your customer. I know it for a fact - I sat in on more than one thousand of your presentations!"

I would estimate that the majority of customers have four times as many buying strategies as most salespeople have selling strategies!

Here's something I'm sure you will be interested in...

How to make the sale even if the competition has lower prices, higher quality and better service

It's hard to believe that the gross profit can range from under 14% to over 21% FOR THE EXACT SAME PRODUCTS!

Here's what more than 500 customers dislike about your salespeople...

Finally! An effective, affordable and efficient sales program based on the scientific system for learning that Ben Franklin devised to acquire the essential principles of success!

7 Fatal Mistakes Many Distributors Are Making

How do you make the sale when your competitor is cheaper on the exact same item made by the exact same manufacturer and is delivered on a truck exactly like yours?

Will chains rule the restaurant business in the future?

Personalize, and be specific!

You can throw the teachings of your English teachers out the window, and the rules of "third person, singular" or whatever else tends to inhibit your writing. **Whenever you sit down to write sales copy intended to pull the orders - sell the product - you should picture yourself in a one-on-one situation and "talk" to your reader just as if you are sitting across from him at your dining room table.** *Say what you mean* and sell HIM or HER on the product you're offering. Be **specific** and ask if these are the things that bother him or her - are these the things he or she wants?

It's also important that you don't get cute with a lot of unrelated graphics and artwork.

Your sales letter should convey the feeling of **excitement** and movement but should not tire the eyes or disrupt the flow of the message you're trying to present. Any graphics or artwork you use should be *relevant to your product*, its use and/or the copy you've written about it.

Graphics should not be used as artistic touches, or to create an atmosphere. Any **illustrations** with your sales letter should *compliment the selling of your product* and prove or substantiate specific points in your copy.

An idea is sold not necessarily when you go into your close, but when the buyer agrees with your statements - and that is what you are looking for - **buyer commitment**.

Your prospect is **indifferent**. They are thinking about themselves, their problems, their goals, and are *completely uninterested* in you or your interruption in their day.

Your prospects are exposed to as many as **three thousand advertising messages every day**. In addition to being interrupted every eight minutes with some type of problem, phone call or employee, they are being called on by hundreds of salespeople.

The first ten seconds...

We have to say something or show the customer something that will pique their interest in such a way that will make them forget all the things that are currently occupying their mind. What can you do or say that will accomplish this important step in the sale; getting attention? Here are a few examples:

♦ Product cost

♦ Labor cost

♦ Increasing customer base

- Increasing order size

- New ideas to help build business

- Marketing and merchandising ideas

- New products or services

- Success stories

- Their profit and loss statement

- Solutions to their potential or current problems

All are good for getting attention.

Turn and point to any person within your vision.

That individual is dominated for the time being with a particular ATTITUDE. This **attitude** is controlling their entire personality. It is coloring their mental and emotional life. They see you through this attitude. Anything you say to them must be sifted through the screen of this fixed ATTITUDE before you can get a spark of interest in what you are talking about.

I don't think I exaggerate when I say that ninety eight percent of the sales letters written are mishandled in the first crucial step.

When your prospect reads your first sentence you are up against an attitude as closed as a barn door.

What can you say that will swing the prospects attitude so they will *read with interest* what you have to say? You MUST have an opening line that breaks through that attitude and provokes the prospect to say...

"Wow, I'll read your story. This is relevant to me and my problems and the goals I am trying to reach! Whoever wrote this letter really knows **ME** and understands **MY** problems!"

You must be specific and talk directly to them, NOT to their organization or company.

Why YOU read a sales letter

When someone has the tools to help you succeed and their main purpose is to provide those tools for your use and help you achieve your goals, it is impossible not to feel the desire to read what they have to say.

When you have your reader's attention, the only way you're going to keep it, is by quickly and emphatically telling him or her what you or your product will do for them.

Don't make the mistake that many sales copywriters make,

the mistake of exaggerating. When you are selling an idea or trying to convince someone of something, you may be tempted to over exaggerate your claims. To get your idea across you may feel you have to use overworked headlines such as:

"We are number one..."
"We are the best in the business..."
"We will get you the best results..."

As soon as one of these statements is made a red flag goes up in the buyer's mind. In your headline you have just "**UNSOLD**" yourself.

The buyer, customer or person you are trying to convince knows immediately that you are stretching the truth.

The buyer (I refer to anyone you are trying to get to buy into your idea, product or service as a "buyer") has three questions:

1. "So what?"
2. "What's in it for me?"
3. "Can you prove it?"

Instead of using the above overworked phrases you should use...

~facts and benefits

~figures

~and examples

in your sales copy to justify your statements. These facts make the buyer *willing to accept you and your offer*.

Your goal is to weave the facts into the sales copy that makes the buyer understand the LEGITIMACY of what you are saying.   Like a shrewd attorney, you want to present your facts in the strongest possible light.

For example:

"Our program will increase your profits by 6% - here is how."

"This product line will cut your labor cost by 3% - I have the facts right here to prove what I am saying."

"This new marketing system will increase your sales by at least 5% - let me show you what I mean"

They really don't care

They don't care how long it's taken you to produce the product, how long you've been in business, nor how many years you've spent learning your craft. He or she wants to know specifically how HE or SHE is going to BENEFIT from the purchase of your product, your service or your speech.

Even though you have your reader's attention, you must follow through with an *enumeration of the benefits he or she can gain*. Mentally picture your prospect - determine their wants and emotional needs - put yourself in their shoes, and ask yourself **'If I were reading this letter, what are the things that would appeal to me?'**

Write your copy to APPEAL to your reader's wants and emotional needs.

VISUALIZE your prospect, recognize his or her wants and satisfy them.

Writing good sales copy is knowing "who" your buyers are; recognizing what he or she wants; and then telling them how your product or service will fulfill each of those wants.

Remember this because it's one of the "vitally important" keys to writing sales copy that does the job you intend for it to do.

It's vitally necessary that you present **"proven facts"** about your product because survey results show that most of the people reading your sales letter - especially those reading it for the first time - **WILL TEND TO QUESTION ITS**

AUTHENTICITY.

So, the more **facts** you can present in the sales letter, the more **credible** your offer. Whether it's an actual sale letter, webpage or email.

And the more **facts** about the product you present, the more **product** you'll sell or services you will provide.

People want facts as reasons, and/or excuses for buying a product - to justify to themselves and others, that they haven't been "taken" by a slick copywriter.

Your letter has to build _belief and credibility_ in the mind of your prospect.

It has to assure him or her of their good judgment in the final decision to hire you - furnish evidence of the benefits you've promised - _and afford them a "safety net" in case anyone should question their decision to hire you_.

Let him or her imagine the RESULTS of hiring you

Induce him or her to **visualize** all of the **benefits** you've promised.

Give them the keys to seeing himself or herself richer, enjoying luxury, having time to do whatever he'd like to do, and with all of his dreams fulfilled.

For example, one of my programs:

A 90-day program that will jumpstart your sales team and provide everything you need to exceed your sales and gross profit goals.

In just 90-days you can be enjoying these benefits...

Increased sales

Increased income

More job security

Higher gross profits

More personal recognition

Praise from your sales team

More respect from upper management

More appreciation from everyone in the company

This can be handled in one or two sentences, or spelled out in a paragraph or more, but it's the **absolute ingredient** you must include to close the sale.

Study all the sales presentations you've ever heard - look at every winning ad - is the element included in all of them that actually makes the sale to you?

Remember it, use it, and don't try to sell anything without it.

Every one of the fundamentals are necessary.

Those people who are easy to sell may perhaps be sold even if some of these factors are left out, but it's wiser to plan your advertisement so it will have a powerful impact upon those who are "hardest" to sell, for, unlike face-to-face selling, we cannot in printed advertising or internet marketing come to a "trial close" in our sales talk - in order to see if those who are easier to sell will welcome the dotted line without further persuasion.

We must assume that we are talking to the hardest ones - and that the more thoroughly our copy sells both the hard and the easy, the better chance we have against the competition for the business.

Demand action from the reader

Lots of ads are beautiful, almost perfectly written, and quite convincing - yet THEY FAIL TO ASK FOR OR DEMAND ACTION FROM THE READER.

If you want the reader to have your product, then tell him so and request that he send his money now.

Unless you enjoy entertaining your prospects with your beautiful writing skills, always demand that he or she complete the sale now, **by acting now - by calling a telephone number and ordering, or by writing his check and rushing it to the post office, or going to your website.**

Once you've got him on the hook, land him!

Don't let him get away.

Probably, one of the most common and best methods of moving the readers to act now is written in some form of the following:

All of this can be yours! You can start enjoying this new way of life immediately, simply by sending a check for $XX! Don't put it off, then later wish you had gotten in on the ground floor. Make out that check now, and "be IN on the ground floor!" Act now, and as an "early-bird" buyer, we'll include a big bonus package - absolutely free, simply for acting immediately! You win all the way! We take all the risks. If you're not satisfied, simply return the product and we'll quickly refund your money! Do it now! Get that check on its way to us today and receive the big bonus package! After next week, we won't be able to include the bonus as a part of this fantastic deal, so act now! The sooner you act, the more you win!

Offering a reward of some kind will almost always stimulate the prospect to act.

However, in mentioning the reward or bonus, be very careful that you don't end up receiving primarily requests for the bonus with mountains of requests for refunds on the product to follow.

The bonus should be mentioned only casually if you're asking for product orders; and with lots of fanfare only when you're seeking inquiries.

Too often the copywriter, in his or her enthusiasm to pull in a record number of responses, confuses the reader by "forgetting about the product," and devoting his entire space allotted for the "demand for action" to sending for the bonus.

Any reward offered should be closely related to the product, and a bonus offered only for immediate action on the part of the potential buyer.

Specify a time limit.

Tell your prospect that he must act within a certain time limit or lose out on the bonus, face probably higher prices, or even the withdrawal of your offer.

This is always a good hook to get action.

Any kind of guarantee you offer always helps to produce action from the prospect.

And the more liberal you can make your guarantee, the more product orders you'll receive.

Be sure you state the guarantee clearly and simply. Make it so easy to understand that even a child would not misinterpret what you're saying.

The action you want your prospect to take should be easy - clearly stated - and devoid of any complicated procedural steps on his part, or numerous directions for him to follow.

Picture your prospect, very comfortable in his favorite easy chair, idly flipping through a magazine while "half-watching" TV.

He notices your ad, reads through it, and he's sold on your product.

Now what does he do?

Remember, he's very comfortable - you've "grabbed" his attention, sparked his interest, painted a picture of him enjoying a new kind of satisfaction, and he's ready to buy.

Anything and everything you ask or cause him to do is going to disrupt this aura of comfort and contentment.

Whatever he must do had better be simple, quick and easy!

Tell him without any ifs, ands or buts, what to do - fill out the coupon, include your check or credit card information for the full amount, and send it in to us today!

Make it as easy for him as you possibly can – *simple and direct.*

And by all means, make sure your address is on the order form he's supposed to complete and mail into you - your name and address on the order form, as well as just above it.

People sometimes fill out a coupon, tear it off, seal it in an envelope and don't know where to send it.

The easier you make it for the prospect to respond, the more responses you'll get!

By conscientiously studying good advertising copy, and practice in writing ads of your own, now that you have the knowledge and understand what makes advertising copy work, you should be able to quickly develop your copyrighting abilities to produce order-pulling ads for your own products.

Even so, and once you do become proficient in writing ads for your own products, you must never stop "noticing" how ads are written, designed and put together by other people.

To stop learning would be comparable to shutting yourself off from the rest of the world.

The best ad writers are people in touch with the world in which they live.

Every time they see a good ad, they clip it out and save it.

Regularly, they pull out these files of good ads and study them, always analyzing what makes them good, and why they work.

There's no school in the country that can give you the same kind of education and expertise so necessary in the field of ad writing.

You must keep yourself up-to-date, aware of, and in-the-know about the other guy - his innovations, style changes, and the methods he's using to sell his products.

On-the-job-training - study and practice - that's what it takes - and if you've got that burning ambition to succeed, you can do it too!

The means to a sale

The toughest thing to realize is that writing is not an end in itself-it's the means to a sale.

Copywriting is one-way communication.

All questions the reader may ask should be anticipated and answered, and there should be specific directions for the reader to follow.

If you want the readers to send for your catalog, buy your product or visit your business, say so.

You've got to have a dynamic, spectacular ad, sales letter or brochure that attracts the eye and grabs the interest of the people you're trying to sell to.

Unless your ad really "jumps out" at the reader, your sales won't live up to expectations, and your ad money will be wasted.

Stress the benefits of your product or service.

Explain to your reader how owning a copy of your book (for instance), or receiving your services will make his life richer, happier, and more abundant.

Don't get involved in detailing all the money you've spent developing the product or researching the information you're selling, or your credentials for offering it.

Stress the "sizzle" and value of ownership.

It is important to involve the reader as often as possible through the use of the word "you."

Write your copy just as if you were speaking to and attempting to sell just one person.

Don't let your ad sound as a speaker at a podium addressing a huge stadium filled with people, but as if there were just one individual "listening."

Don't try to be overly clever, brilliant or humorous.

Keep your copy simple, to the point, and on target toward selling your prospect the product or service because of its benefits.

In other words, keep it simple, but clear. You don't want to confuse the reader.

Just tell him exactly what he'll get for his money; the benefits he'll receive; how to go about ordering it.

You don't have to get too friendly.

In fact, avoid becoming "folksy," and don't use slang expressions.

In writing ad copy, think of yourself as a door-to-door salesperson.

You have to get the attention of the prospect quickly, interest him or her in the product you're selling, create a desire to enjoy its benefits, and you can then close the sale.

A good exercise is to study your competition and recognize how they are selling their wares.

Practice rewriting their ads from a different point of view or from a different sales angle.

Keep a file of ads you've clipped from different publications in a file of ad writing ideas.

Don't copy anyone else's work word for word; just use the ad material of others to stimulate your own creativeness.

If you're making offers via direct mail, best get into the postal system with it on a Sunday, Monday or Tuesday, to be sure it does not arrive on a Monday, the first and busiest day of the week.

Unless you're promoting a big-ticket item, the quality or color of your paper won't have any great effect on the response you'll get, but the quality of your printing definitely will, so bear this in mind when you place your printing order.

The summer months when people are most apt to be away on vacation are usually not good months for direct mail.

But they are good for opportunity advertisements in publications often found in vacation areas, and in motels and hotels.

Some people brag about their luck in having not one but several "in" seasons, each about 30 days long.

For example, the wristwatch and candy seasons, with their sudden glorious agency-inspired campaigns to attract buyers who remember such recipients as dads, grads, moms, and brides.

They spend with seemingly unlimited budgets on advertising; then they lay low until the next "in" season-Christmas, Easter, or St. Patrick's Day.

No one should allow his selling season to be shorter than 365 days in any calendar year or allow ad funds to run dry before they have somehow touched each of its 52 weeks.

Again, it cannot be stressed too much or too often: Success in marketing does, indeed, depend upon advertising - and as with anything else, quality pays off in the long run.

Read this information carefully; study it; let it sink in.

Then apply the principles outlined in it.

They have worked for others, and THEY CAN WORK FOR YOU!

To successfully sell your products and services you must understand the principles of _persuasive writing._

You must know a **feature from a benefit** as well as everything there is to know about the product and the people you want to buy it.

The following questions will help put the product or service in focus before you do any writing.

• Do you have a price advantage or a price problem?

• If you do not have an advantageous price, don't say a thing about price.

• Make sure that your benefits are strong enough to get people interested so that when you follow up directly they will be sufficiently interested to pay a higher price.

• If you do have a price advantage, let your readers know.

• You may not want to include the actual price in the brochure or advertisement, but you can make many sales points just by saying that your product sells for less.

• Who is the person who will buy your product or service?

There's no substitute for actually talking with prospects and customers to see what motivates them to buy your products or those of your competitors.

Too much advertising is totally wasted because the advertisers never know anything about the people who buy the products.

If you dig deep enough, the reasons people buy will emerge.

Be sure that you know whom you want to influence.

Every situation is different, and you can make the most of your advertising and marketing dollars if you write to the audience that can be most influential in the sale.

The economic benefits

If you can say that your product or service will _save the customer money, time, or effort,_ you have a great competitive advantage. If you can document this with figures, you'll have a very persuasive story to tell.

Don't be afraid to go into the details.

If your customer is even the least bit cost conscious, they will read every word of your copy.

What is the product made of or what does the service consist of?

Carefully detail the product or service you are going to market.

If it is a product, get all the details on how it is made, what it is made of, etc.

If it is a service, describe exactly what the service consists of.

Write out the description as if you were explaining it to a young child who knew absolutely nothing about it.

Your features and benefits

All products have several features and benefits that will appeal to prospects.

Before you write a word, determine which of the benefits will be most important to the largest segment of your market.

Keep in mind that a **feature** is a **fact** about the product or service and a benefit is what the feature will do for the customer.

People buy benefits, not features.

Your competitive differences?

Your product or service may be better than that of a competitor on a point that doesn't make any real difference to the person who must make the choice.

Don't be fooled into using this advantage as a benefit.

Even if you do have a great competitive advantage over

other products, never knock the competitors.

But do make sure that your reader knows the difference and appreciates what it will mean if your product is bought.

Where and how to buy

Once you get people interested enough in your product or service to either want more information or to buy it, you will have to tell them where and how it can be bought.

If you're trying to sell directly from the ad, tell the readers how much to send and where to send their money.

If you're using salespeople, reps, or distributors, let them know who their local sales agent is.

Don't leave anything to chance.

It may seem as though "call now for information" or "send for free catalog" is too obvious, however few people will call unless you tell them to.

When you know everything about the product that can affect the sale, you can begin to think about the copy itself.

But, before you put any words on paper, there are a few

points you should think about.

People who have never written advertising tend to think more in terms of gimmicks and tricks than they do of the importance of creating a sales message.

Don't think that you have to trick your prospects into reading your ad.

 If you give the readers the information, they want you are on your way to a sale.

This is not a pick-and-choose list.

If you skip any point your copy will be weak.

State the objectives.

Your first job is to determine just what you want to accomplish. Here are the objectives most often associated with advertising copy:

a. To introduce a new product or service or a new feature of an existing one.

b. To explain unique characteristics of your product or service.

c. To explain the performance or your product or service.

d. To show how the product or service deliveries results.

e. To initiate an immediate reader response.

f. To aid distributors in their sales efforts.

g. To enhance the brand or company image.

h. To tell of company developments that may enhance sales.

i. To tell of price changes, guarantees, discounts, etc.

j. To retain a good image when there are problems.

Choose ONE! Any attempt to feature two or more objectives will weaken your ad.

You can, of course, make other points in your copy, but every piece of copy you write should have one major objective, and there should be no doubt in the reader's mind what you are trying to say.

Describe your customer

When you know your readers and what they will respond to,

you can write the kind of copy that will attract their attention.

It means that each respond more favorably when you use language that is familiar.

Know when the product is purchased.

Timing can be an important issue when advertising and promoting your products or services. Is there a specific time of the week, month or year that can affect the sale?

Know how the product is bought.

If your product is usually bought in certain units, and there are advantages to your way of offering the products, the facts should be included.

And your readers will want to know how you plan to sell to them.

Company salespeople?

Reps?

Distributors?

Direct mail?

Visit the store or web site?

Home demonstration?

Know why the product is bought.

Don't limit your search for why a product is bought to the usual points such as price, quality, etc.

Find additional reasons.

Decide exactly what you want the reader to do.

If you want them to send for a catalog, say so.

Tell them to call or write.

Decide before you write anything that this is where you want to take the reader after he or she has finished reading your ad or brochure.

If you write with this in mind, your request won't look as though it was tacked on as an afterthought.

List every feature and every benefit.

Start with the features, the facts about the product or service.

List them in a single column, and then list the benefits in a second column.

There will be more than one benefit for each feature.

Don't give up until you are absolutely sure that you have every benefit, and that you know which benefits will be most important to most of the people who will read your copy.

Not all the benefits will be used, but you should list them before you start writing.

Decide the order in which you will present your benefits.

Actually, once you have made your major point, the order in which you present your benefits will make very little difference.

However, there is a little trick you can use to make sure that your readers don't try to rank order the points when you don't want them to.

Never use numbers when you list benefits.
   Place a bullet next to each just to separate them.
   Decide on the copy style.

Straight explanation is the most effective style, not because it is necessarily most effective, but because it's usually the easiest to handle.

Your points of difference

It's true! You can't sell anybody anything, you can't change people's minds, you can't persuade them to do something against their will and you can't get people to buy based on price alone.

We have to be crystal clear about what our job really is. We think that we have to apply pressure, use special psychological techniques and force people to buy from us.

Regardless of whether you are a supervisor, a sales person, a waitress, a service provider or a marketing manager your job is the same: Your job is to help people make good decisions - and the more informed you are about your products and services, the more valuable you are to your customer.

You can make your life a whole lot easier starting right now by stop thinking that you have to be clever and use some secret selling technique to get people to buy from you. All you have to do is answer this question; Why should I buy from you? When someone asks that question of you what they are really asking is "I need help making a good decision!"

You might sell the exact same thing as everyone else, but you point out the differences of why your product or service is unique to their business. Sure, everyone else is selling the same thing; however, what makes yours different is you have asked your clients about what they want from the product. You have listened and taken notes and figured out what your customer is trying to accomplish. You then give the customer the solution to their problem. The best part is, it has not cost you anything because you are not charging extra, just helping the customer make a good decision. You are adding value.

The "point of difference" of your product is the extra service you offer. This extra, in a sense, is your consulting service. And as a customer, when I can get free consulting service with a product or service the decision of who to buy from is easy. Even if it is a meal in a restaurant.

The secret of persuading people is that there is no secret. Just call on enough people and show them why doing business with you is the best decision they can possibly make! And if everything is equal, the deciding factor will be the fact that YOU go with the deal.

How am I supposed to learn everything about the products I sell when there is so much confusing information that I have to muddle through?

The answer - points of difference.

To increase your product knowledge, compare points of difference in the products. Each point of difference can be viewed as positive or negative depending on what your customer is looking for. Each point will change the price and the value of the product.

Considering the number of line items, it takes to maintain a competitive inventory, gaining sufficient product knowledge is a long, slow process. With new products and programs being introduced continuously and old ones being changed or discontinued, it becomes a real challenge to stay on top of the necessary information.

The secret of gaining product knowledge is to compare points of difference. What is the difference between the new and the old? What is the difference between your product and a competitor's product? Each point of difference will change the price and the value of the product.

As a professional copywriter you must be able to sell value added products. What kind of definition would you come up with when you are asked the meaning of "Value Added Selling"?

The best answer is to know the points of difference and sell your differences as a benefit.

A salesperson who can answer objections with good solid facts and product information will outperform the person who "wings it" every time.

To gain the respect of your customers and earn their business, product knowledge should be a daily activity.

To increase product knowledge continually ask questions that help customers make the right choices. Read the trade journals and clip articles that contain helpful information for your customers.

All product knowledge has to be translated into customer benefits if it is to be of value to the customer. When selling, it does little good to focus on the features of the products or services offered. It makes little difference how long your company has been in business, how large your facility is, or how many employees you have unless it can be used to solve your customers problems.

Here is how you might use this to raise the bar on your own services. Take out any one of your software boxes or stop in the computer store and browse through the software department. Notice how they are always comparing the old version with the new upgraded version. What would an upgraded version of YOU look like? What points of difference would there be between the old you and the you that you will become with just a slight nudge?

Here are a few examples:

The old version of you compared to the new version of you

OLD - Ho-hum about what I do
NEW - Really excited about my profession

OLD - Take care of my customers
NEW - Give extraordinary customer service

OLD - Only put in enough effort to get buy
NEW - Always go the extra mile for every customer

OLD - Customers know I appreciate them
NEW - Go out of my way to say thanks and show appreciation for my customers

When selling yourself and your services you must be able to convince your prospective customer that you are the right choice, you must know your strengths and be sure you transmit them, so the message is received. Your customers can buy products from anyone. Today, everyone is selling the same products. The most important point of difference is you. YOU are the customer's link to the universe. YOU are the one thing that really makes a difference. This puts a responsibility on you to be resource - a problem solver. A typical person trying to make a sale focuses on price while a true marketer finds out from the customer what he or she wants and helps them get it.

Ask yourself this question. How much could I get someone to pay me to listen to my sales pitch? Most likely the answer is zero. However, consultants get paid thousands of dollars an hour to do what? Ask questions.

Why you lose business

What is the easiest way for a competitor to take a customer away from you? Why do you lose accounts to your competitors?

Here are some reasons that sound good: Our service isn't up to par. Our prices are too high. We have too many out-of-stocks. My competitor is better known in my market.

I have a surprise for you. When you lose an account, it is mostly due to one reason. I would say that 95% of all the accounts you lose to a competitor are for this single reason! This single reason will enable you to take away more business from your competitor than you can handle.

It's easier than you think. Here's why. Your competitors are taking their customers for granted. I guarantee it! Let me say that again in capital letters...

YOUR COMPETITORS ARE TAKING THEIR CUSTOMERS FOR GRANTED.

And do you know what else? So, are you - I know, I know - you don't want to hear that? It's true - you know it and I know it.

Let's put it to the test. Do you feel appreciated? Probably not. Would you like a little appreciation?   If your answer is yes - you are not alone. In a recent survey 6,600 people were asked two questions:

1. Do you receive as much praise, recognition and appreciation as you feel you deserve?

6,415 SAID NO

2. Would you perform your job better if you were given more praise, recognition and appreciation?

6,495 SAID YES

This, of course, doesn't apply to you - you are in sales - it is up to you to GIVE appreciation not GET it. The point is - most people feel unappreciated.

Here's more proof - a real life example: I was helping a small foodservice distributor look for a way to promote their business. We thought about a food show, however, due to the small size of the company we felt that it would be too big of an undertaking. After a lot of talking we finally came up with a program we called a "customer appreciation dinner."

We contacted 20 of his suppliers and asked them to participate by serving dinner to the customers and at the same giving them the opportunity to show samples of their products. All the suppliers agreed, and we put together a buffet line concept with the theme being that we want to show our customers that we appreciate their business.

We decided to use an RSVP format so we would know how many people would show up, and we could tell the suppliers how many people they could plan on feeding. We arranged to have the dinner at a Holiday Inn with a room large enough to hold 108 people at one time.

We sent out 525 invitations expecting to get about 200 RSVP's. The invitation said, "When was the last time someone took you to dinner to show you how much they appreciate your business?"

Not knowing the power of our theme, "Customer Appreciation Dinner", we had 525 RSVP's! We had to turn the tables FIVE TIMES during the evening. Every restaurant in the small southern town was closed with a sign on the door saying "Closed - we went out for dinner."

The normal procedure is to get an account, wine and dine them during the honeymoon period, and then put them on auto pilot. You are guilty of it, aren't you? Admit it.

How can you take away business from a competitor? Here's the secret. Get a small order from your competitor's customer and then show that you REALLY appreciate their business. Too simple? - You WILL stand out and be noticed.

Sure, you gave the customer a discount - THEY should appreciate YOU! Your customer is the one who writes out those big checks every week - they are not thinking about how much they appreciate the small discount they got - they are wondering if YOU appreciate the amount of business, THEY are giving YOU.

Your customers pay your mortgage, put your kids through school, make your car payments, pay for your retirement plan. Your top twenty customers - Do you thank them enough? Do you show them that you appreciate their business? More than likely the answer is no.

Give your customers the attention and appreciation they are hungry for. Give your prospects the attention and appreciation they are not getting from their current supplier and you will take away the business.

Few things are more gratifying than gratitude, and very few

business owners express their gratitude as much as they should.

Appreciation can go a lot farther than just saying thank you. How many thank you notes did you send last year? Your competitors are not doing it. It's the little messages of gratitude that will make a big difference.

I was sitting in a buyer's office when a fax came in for him. He seemed a little upset, so I asked him if there was anything wrong. He said a salesman had just left with a large order and he just faxed a thank you note.

I thought that was pretty good for a salesperson to take the time to send a thank you fax. However, the buyer said he was going to cancel the order, but because of the thank you note it became too difficult to call and cancel.

You never know what insurance your thank you notes, follow up phone calls and extra attention is providing. Here is more proof.

Headquarters wanted to know why a small pizza shop was performing way beyond everyone's expectations. They were number one in a large national chain – yet located in a small town with a lot of competition.   When they investigated, they found that before closing they would go through their deliveries and call everyone to make sure their pizza was good!

CAN YOU IMAGINE THAT? A thank you call from a PIZZA SHOP.

I just bought a new house. After the closing I never heard a peep from the broker - nothing - zero! I even had to call his office and tell them to come and get their sign out of my yard!

No - Service is not the reason you lose business.

No - Price is not the reason you lose business.

No - Your competitor's image in the market is not the reason.

No - it's none of those things.

The reason you lose, on average TWENTY-FIVE PERCENT OF YOUR BUSINESS EVERY YEAR is because you didn't listen to your mother when she told you to say, "Thank You."

Building customer relationships

What has caused you, in the past, to think about the possibility of doing something besides selling? Here is the answer. The indifferent, reluctant, defensive attitude that greets you every time you make a sales call is what defeats nearly everyone who fails in a selling career.

Wouldn't it be nice if you were welcomed everywhere you went? If potential customers said "yes, come in, tell me more?"

What can you do or say that will make a prospect treat you favorably? How can you get them to change from indifference and reluctance to being receptive and looking at your products and services?

Here is the answer. Changing their attitude starts by managing your attitude (ATTITUDE MANAGEMENT). You have to continue to feel good about them even if they don't feel good about you, or themselves.

Not as easy as it sounds. Keep in mind that you are not selling products and services, you are selling yourself.

If your company comes out with a new product you can be sure every competitor is finding out how it can be duplicated. The same goes for services. Come out with a new way of providing extra services and you will have an edge for a while. However, it won't be long before a competitor will be offering the same service.

Adding extra services without increasing your price is actually lowering your gross profit. As one president of a large distribution company said, "All I really have is a warehouse full of commodities."

If the difference is the personal relationship you can establish with your customers, what can you do to enhance that relationship? To answer this question all you have to do is ask what makes you like or dislike someone you are doing business with?

You like people who like you. Someone who is interested in all aspects of your business. Someone who talks about the things you want and the goals you are trying to accomplish.

Here is the secret of getting past their indifference. Here is what would make YOU buy from someone. When someone has the tools to help you succeed and their main purpose is to provide those tools for your use and help you achieve your goals, it is impossible not to feel the desire to work with them.

Let's say that again... it is important.

When someone has the tools to help YOU succeed and their main purpose is to provide those tools for YOUR use and help YOU achieve YOUR goals, it is IMPOSSIBLE not to feel the desire to work with them.

Most of the time customers and prospects don't know what they want. You, as a sales consultant, have to help your customers identify their goals and show them you are interested in helping them succeed.

Sounds altruistic, I know. But consider this - as one very successful marketer put it when asked why he did so much for his customers, why he always went the extra mile and always put his customers first; "because I am a very selfish person. I like to make money."

Another benefit of this "altruistic" approach - it gets your mind off of yourself and you lose your fear.

Getting customers to care

Sometimes you have to take a negative approach to get a positive response, sometimes you have to be creative to get someone's attention in the first place, and sometimes you have to really think outside the box to make people take notice.

I am going to give you an example that is going to blow your mind. But first, let me show you a couple of things I have in my files that really seem to work, and some that don't.

Whenever I am on an airplane or in a crowd of strangers, I am asked what I do. According to the experts you should have an "elevator speech" for these occasions. You should be able to tell people what you do by the time the elevator makes it from one floor to the next.

I designed a clever 30 second speech and it really seemed to turn people off. As soon as I said I was a "sales trainer" I could see the expression on their face turn to panic. They immediately said they don't use sales trainers, or they have a company employee who does their sales training. They had a readymade objection. So, by following the advice of the experts, I was turning people off in less than 30 seconds.

Back to the drawing board. I took a different approach by thinking outside the box.

I created a "shock" effect and I am now able to get people's interest and have some fun at the same time. Now, when they ask me what I do, here is what I say:

"I show people how to stay 4 steps ahead of the sheriff, would you like to know what those 4 steps are?" And they always say YES?

I give them four quick steps that would be applicable to them and ask which step would be most helpful. If they say "step 3" I give them a really good sound bite of information on step 3. I then get their business card and follow up with some more helpful information.

I am getting ready to do a 5,000-piece mailing and guess what will be on the envelope? You got it: "How to stay 4 steps ahead of the sheriff, would you like to know what the 4 steps are?"

When you are approaching a new account think of your first few words as the sales copy on the envelope. The job of the sales copy is NOT to make the sale, but to get them OPEN UP!

Here are some of the standard openers and my translation. If you are guilty you might spend a little time creating something that works for you. Be easy on yourself, everyone has used them.

"I am sorry for interrupting."

Translation: I really don't amount to much - you are much more important than I am - you see I am just a doormat waiting for someone to wipe their feet on me.

"I know you are busy."

Translation: I really don't have any respect for you or your time - you are a busy and important person and I am intruding in you day.

"I was in the neighborhood."

Translation: I am not very organized - I simply drift through my day from neighborhood to neighborhood making random calls on people and waste their time.

"Do you need anything?"

Translation. I am really not much of a salesperson and I was wondering if there are any crumbs left over from a real sales person who has been here.

"I wanted to stop by and introduce myself."

Translation. I am really not ambitious enough to have done some homework about you so I guess I will tell you all about ME.

I think you get the point. Things are different out there today, so you have to be different or they eat you alive.

Today's customers are being bombarded with an estimated 3,000 sales and marketing messages every day. How do you stand out and set yourself apart from the crowd? You have to hit them with a HUGE BENEFIT. A benefit that will have the same power as if you hit them between the eyes with a baseball bat!

How should you make your entrance into an account?

First: Attitude. You should always assume an attitude of confidence and purpose. Never apologize for making the call. Never feel like you are interrupting.   Never say, "I was in the neighborhood" as if your call was not important. Never say, "I wanted to stop by and introduce myself." Who cares?

There is a psychological law that makes the prospect react and respond to the attitude and action expressed by you the salesperson.   There is nothing complicated about it, except the results that come when you put this psychological law into effect. Make the call with confidence.

Second. A huge SPECIFIC BENEFIT.   For example.: "I am here to show you how you can lower your operating expenses by $5,323 dollars per quarter -or- I am here to show you how increase your invoice size by 25 cents, which equates to $813 per week, let me show you how I figured it based on your current volume -or- I have a product that will cut your cleaning time by 23% resulting in a labor cost savings of $103 per week or $5,356 per year."

I can hear you now.   "But Bob, I have to call on my accounts every week!" How could I possibly come up with a new money saving or money-making idea for my customers EVERY WEEK?"

My answer. How many line items do you have? 2,000? 4,000? 8,000? 10,000?   Every line item you have in your inventory represents an opportunity. How many services do you have? 27? 37? 47? Or how about 57?

I can still hear you. "But Bob, all my competitors are selling on price and I have to meet their prices or lose the business."

What if your competitor was giving their product away FREE? What if there was very little quality difference between your product and the "free" product? What if their method of distribution was much more efficient than yours? Could you sell against that kind of competition? No?

Well someone was given a sales challenge to sell against that kind of market condition. And they are very successful. The product is bottled water. How do they do it? Do they lower their price and try to compete with tap water? Do they badmouth the water company and tell their customers "yea, it may be free, but look at what you get!"

Is bottled water really any better? I gave it the ultimate taste test. I put two bowls of water in front of my dog – one from a bottle that I paid over a dollar for – the other from the sink faucet. My dog tried both of them. Which one do you think she preferred? The tap water! Did I switch to tap water? No. I still pay an outrageous price for a bottle of water.

Why? Somehow the perceived value of water in a bottle is a strong enough benefit for me to fork over my hard-earned cash.

Every item in your warehouse has within it a huge benefit to the customer or it wouldn't be in the warehouse. All you have to do is find ONE BENEFIT PER WEEK and present it to all your customers.

Let's do the math. Thirty-five accounts x one benefit per week x 52 weeks = 1,820 benefit presentations per year.

Even a blind hog can find an acorn once in a while. If you make ONE THOUSAND EIGHT HUNDRED AND TWENTY benefit presentations per year – you will sell something – even if by accident.

The bottom line. You walk into your account. There have been 2,999 people trying to sell this person today and you are number 3,000.

Do you say – "I'm sorry for interrupting?"

Do you say – "I know you are busy?"

Do you say – "I was in the neighborhood?"

Do you say – "Do you need anything?"

Do you say – "I wanted to stop by and introduce myself?"

Only if you want the customer to say – "Who cares?"

Instill confidence

Years ago, there was an essay written about government. The title of the essay was "The Fox Knew Many Things, But the Hedgehog Knew One Big Thing."

I never read the essay, but the title has a good message for us in sales.

We all have some fox in us and know a lot of things, but to be successful in today's competitive market and really build your level of confidence you must know ONE BIG THING.

It's easy to get sidetracked and become like the fox, who knows all types of things, but here's the problem with knowing all types of things, you will not be KNOWN for anything. To have total confidence with your customers your ONE BIG THING must be crystal clear in their mind as well as yours. You must be looked upon as an expert.

If I am buying insurance, I want to buy from a confident person who's ONE BIG THING is insurance. I want to deal with someone who "wrote the book" on insurance.

If I am buying or selling a house, I want to deal with a

confident person whose ONE BIG THING is real estate, NOT someone who is a dental assistant "thinking of getting into real estate on the side!"

If I am buying a car, I want the salesperson's ONE BIG THING to be knowledge of the car. If I ask how wide the car's wheelbase is, I want them to know without him or her having to look it up.

If I own a restaurant, I want to buy from someone whose ONE BIG THING is selling food and who has a passion for the restaurant business. Someone who can identify with me and "knows where I am coming from."

The biggest reason most salespeople fail is that they never decide that SELLING is their one big thing. They never make the do-or-die decision that THIS IS IT. Once you make that decision and stop thinking about what else you could be doing, sales will take off.

What keeps you from making the "do-or-die" decision that will give you that solid feeling that you are in control? There are a lot of ups and downs in selling, and when you have a down day you are at your weakest point. That is when you start to wonder why you have

taken on such a difficult occupation. On the other hand, when you have a good day, you wouldn't trade it for anything.

If you look closely at a sailboat tacking into the wind it looks like it's going back and forth without getting anywhere. If you look at it from a distance, it's easy to see it is heading in a specific direction.

Selling is the same thing. If you look too closely at every presentation, every phone call, every turn-down, it will

seem like you are getting nowhere. If you look at the week, month and quarter, you will see that you are making progress toward your goal.

To have the total respect of your customers you must be committed to be a professional. You must be extreme about your ONE BIG THING. If you spent just 30 minutes a day studying your products and your profession you would eventually be in the top 10% of your industry.

How to establish trust

You are under the gun for more sales. You call on a prospect, dump your sales pitch in their lap and wonder why they don't jump on board with you. You even cut the price so low you are not making any money. They still don't bite. And you wonder how people can be so set in their ways that they won't buy from you.

You start looking for someone to blame. You think that your company doesn't offer the right products, or the service is not good enough. Your prices are too high! All you have to do to see the problem is look in the mirror and ask yourself "why should someone buy from me?" "I'm honest" you might say. "I work for a good company" you might be thinking. "I know my products inside and out" you might be saying, trying to justify your lack of sales.

All those things are important, but they don't matter that much. Just about everyone in sales has the same things going for them. Let's look at it from the prospect's point of view.

"I don't care how low your prices are. I don't care how many benefits you have. I don't care if you have the most perfect offer in the universe. I don't know you - so I don't trust you. Period!" So, Job 1 is to establish trust.

You MUST establish trust if you want to make the sale. And today people don't trust anybody unless they have earned it and neither should you. Here is the one way guaranteed to build trust. And if you are a buyer, don't buy unless you established trust with the person doing the selling. In today's economy, everybody is under the gun. They feel the pressure. The heat is on and some people don't know how to deal with it.

The only way to build trust today is consistent exposure. Consistent exposure means that you make the first call and pick up some information. It means on the second call you pick up a little more information. It means on the third call you bring them an idea that will help their business. On the fourth call, you bring them a sample. On the fifth call, you bring them some helpful news, etc. I know what you are thinking. I need business NOW.

"I just lost one of my biggest accounts." "My income is going to take a huge cut."

Well, you should have thought of that 21 weeks ago. That is how many exposures it takes today before someone will really trust you enough to give you their business. Let me say that again. TWENTY-ONE exposures! Are you so confident that you don't need to call on any new business? Are you so sure about your current customers that you know they will never leave you, never go out of business, never switch ownership or a dozen other reasons that can cause you to lose a customer?

Starting today increase the number of prospects you are calling on. Start now to establish trust so when you lose a customer through no fault of your own, you have a reserve of prospects you can turn up the heat and add them to your active customer base.

Sell on value vs. price

If you don't know the reasons that justify your price, it is important to find out what those reasons are.

The business department of a major university conducted a test on 100 companies. They divided them into three groups according to how they sold.

~ The first group of companies sold strictly on price. The salespeople had as much flexibility as they felt they needed to get the business.

~ The second group of companies was allowed to give heavily controlled price discounts.

~ The third group of companies gave no discounts and sold at book price.

The results...

Group one sold the least amount on a per salesperson basis, earned the less gross profit, return on investment was the poorest in the industry. Price buyers would search for the salespeople who sell on price and try to squeeze the price even lower. The salespeople constantly complained that there was no loyalty among buyers.

Group two had higher quality salesperson than group one, earned a higher gross profit and had a better return on investment. The salespeople complained that if they had lower prices they could sell more.

Group three had the highest per person sales, the highest gross profit and the best return on investment. THE SALESPEOPLE WERE BETTER TRAINED IN SELLING STRATEGIES AND WERE ABLE TO JUSTIFY THEIR PRICE RATHER THAN DISCOUNT IT!

If you are getting beat up on price it is important to find out the reasons that justify the price you are asking. No two products are ever the same even if you are selling against a competitor who is selling the exact same product. You must look at what surrounds the product that makes yours different.

Here are the 8 basic reasons your customers will pay more. Notice that none of these have anything to do with the price.

1) Consistency.

(2) Arrives in Good Condition.

(3) Problems Fixed Quickly.

(4) Operating Cost Savings.

(5) Company Stability.

(6) Fewer Headaches.

(7) Knowledgeable Sales Rep.

(8) Company Reputation.

I am going to make this crystal clear. When you finish reading this you should easily be able to switch your customer from buying on price to buying on value.

Here are some examples that should shift your thinking and show you how to shift the thinking of your customer.

If you have $100 to spend on dinner to celebrate your kids' birthday, what are you going to look for? The best value for your money.

If you have $400 in your budget for a monthly car payment, what are you going to look for? The most car for your payment.

If you have been pre-qualified by the bank to buy a $150,000 house, what are you going to look for? The most house for your money.

If you have 4 kids and a grocery budget of $250 a week,

what are you going to look for? The most value for your money.

If you have decided that you are going to spend $2,000 on a new flat screen TV, what are you going to look for? The most TV for your $2,000.

OK, I know what you are thinking. How can you use this to make the sale instead of cutting the price?

Here is how to make the shift in thinking.

You're selling to a restaurant owner. Here is what you say: "You are spending $5,000 per week for your food, so your goal is to get the most value and the highest quality for your $5,000 weekly investment, is that correct? That is why we don't simply throw out prices and try to beat everyone. We take your budget and give you the highest value for your investment. For example, our service, our quality, our in-stock items, etc.

You're selling staffing services. Here is what you say: "You are paying $18.00 per hour for an employee, so your goal is to get the most value for your $18.00 per hour investment, is that correct? That is why we don't simply try to beat everyone's hourly price. We take your budget and give you the highest value for your investment. For example, here are 57 services we can offer that makes us the best value for your money.

You're selling a training and coaching program. Here is what you say: "I am sure you will agree, $200 per month per person is a very reasonable investment for training and coaching, especially with the results you will get? Here is why our program delivers so much more value for your investment than anything else available: You can continue until your sales are up to where they need to be. Plus, you can miss a session and easily make it up. Plus, we can become your ongoing training partner. Plus, our training is very interactive - NOT a lecture series! Plus, we address your individual selling roadblocks and find solutions! Plus, you can quit anytime if you are not happy and your payments stop! Plus, you can start RIGHT NOW - NO WAITING - GET IMMEDIATE RESULTS! Plus, you can have confidence in our results because we are experts - all we do is sales training! That is more value than any other program available, especially for the small monthly investment, don't you agree?"

You're selling a house. Here is what you say: "I am sure you will agree, the payment on this house is $1,227 per month including taxes and insurance is a stretch. You may be able to find a house with a smaller payment, but look at this street, look at this neighborhood, look at this backyard, how about this great deck, and this fireplace, and these appliances, and the homeowner's warranty, and the association benefits, etc."

You're selling a car. Here is what you say: "What is the payment or price range you are looking for? $400 per month. Then our goal is to find you the best value for your investment, let's start with this one I have right here. It not only has a huge rebate, all the great features, but we have marked it down as well. With all this, you are actually getting a $600 per month car for a $400 per month investment."

Your presentation is helping them make the best decision by showing how much value they will get when they buy from you?

How customers decide

Everybody likes to think of him or herself as a nonconformist, someone who does their own thing. You and I like to see ourselves as independent – until it comes time to decide – then we find out what everybody else is doing and what everybody else thinks – and conclude that they must be right – and make the decision to do the same thing.

Let's say you are a new salesperson calling on a potential account. Would you say; 'I am new and don't have any customers yet – will you take a chance and be the first?" If you were a seasoned salesperson would you go to a potential customer and say; "We have great quality and excellent service?" No, you wouldn't want to say something like that because their response would be "so what." You would want to bring on your success stories, testimonials, references, people your prospect knows and a list of happy customers who are buying from you. Why? To make them feel safe about their decision to buy from you.

Have you ever bought something based on the fact that it was recommended by a friend? Would the statement made by a doctor or dentist give you a little more confidence in the product? How about going to a movie that everyone on your social network was talking about? Would that make you feel more comfortable with your decision? If so, you are not alone. People are highly influenced and persuaded by what others do.

When someone is on trial the defense attorney will bring on witness after witness on the behalf of the defendant. When you hire a real estate person to sell your home you want recommendations from "witnesses" who have hired them.

What does your reputation look like when someone asks for references and testimonials? What does all this mean? It means that this concept works, and it can work for you too.

How?

Bring on your references and testimonials. Call your witnesses to testify on your behalf.

Testimonials work well if the person has the credentials and says something that can be directly related to a benefit for your reader.

The danger in using a testimonial is to end up with brag-and-boast copy, which is always weak.

Some advertisers use cartoons, but this approach is best left to professionals.

You can use humor, but it, too, takes a pro to carry it off.

Many advertisers have found that an ad prepared to look like a newsletter is an effective way to get people to read a lot of copy.

The newsletter copy should contain some news, but don't forget that you are writing to sell.

If you can get your readers involved in more than just reading, you will have done your copy job well.

You have to give them a big, fat, outrageous WOW!!!

How to add value

A sales rep told me how he would go into an account with both a high priced and a low-priced product. He would say that he was reluctant to show the higher priced product and implied that the customer doesn't want this high-quality product. Even though it is the best you can buy, the price is high – much higher than this cheap economy brand. He said that whenever he used this technique the customer seemed to want what the salesperson was reluctant to sell.

Another sales rep recently told me a great story about how to keep from giving a discount or from having to negotiate the price. He was having a brake job done on his car and the cost was $140. When he asked, "Is that the best you can do" here is how he responded: "If you want to negotiate the price – the brake job will cost you $150!"

Think about what a great answer that is. What is he really saying? He is saying that I am already giving you the best price I can. He is saying that if you want to negotiate, I will raise the price to $150 and we can see if you can get me down to the bottom price of $140.

Reluctance is an important tool that can be used in selling. How? If you give a discount too easily or too quickly you have actually cheated the customer out of the feeling that he or she made a good purchase. Have you ever had the feeling that you paid too much for something? Where did that feeling come from? It came from the fact that the salesperson lowered the price too quickly. "Maybe I should have asked for a bigger discount?" You are thinking. "Maybe the salesperson has been overcharging me right along?"

I was sitting on the plane and the woman sitting next to me was in advertising sales. When I asked her what the biggest mistake was that she ever made in sales, here is what she told me. "I was calling on a pawn shop with my sales manager. He told me the bottom-line price was

$1,500 but to try and get $2,000. He said to go down slowly and reluctantly so you "add value" to the program. When the customer asked for the price, I made a huge mistake said $1,500! The customer ended up paying $1,400 and I ended up getting chewed out!"

Here is another reason we should be slightly reluctant when giving a price reduction. My accountant once told me that I should forget the term "gross profit" and replace it with "contribution to overhead". He said that every time I lower the price, I am giving part of the company away! The warehouse cost is 04%, the sales department cost is 04%, the transportation department is another 04%, administration cost is 04% and the bottom line should be at least 04%. When you cut your price below 20% think about what part of the company you are cutting out and giving away!

You don't want to appear too hungry for the sale or too eager to give everything away. When you do a customer will be suspicious and begin to wonder why you are so anxious to make a sale.

Increase add-on sales by 50%

Beware of the person who agrees to your price too quickly, they may plan on asking for more.

If the buyer agrees to your price too quickly there is usually a request that will be close behind.

"That price sounds pretty good, I will take 100 cases." "By the way can I have special terms on that?"

Another customer might agree to the price right away and ask for the same day or next day delivery. From a buyer's perspective, this is called the "add-on."

Agree to the initial price and then as soon as the salesperson starts ringing up their commission, drop the "add-on" question. This is also an excellent strategy for you to use as a salesperson. Once you have what you want in hand, there is a natural tendency to leave as fast as you can. Perhaps there is an unconscious fear that the customer will change their mind or cancel the order - just the opposite is true.

Once a person decides, their mind works to reinforce the decision. By getting a small commitment first the buyer will start to justify the decision and it becomes easier, not harder, to add on additional items.

Why? Think about your own decision-making process. Once you decide your mind does a search, similar to a computer doing a search for additional information. Your mind is looking for ways to justify the decision you just made.

Your customer's mind works the same way. This tactic is being used on you every time you buy a car. First, the car salesperson will get you to agree on the color, then options, then an extended warranty, and before you know it you bought the car - one small piece at a time.

The last-minute add-on involves throwing in an extra request (usually not so huge as to break the sale but big enough to hurt) at the final moment, just when you, the salesperson, have put down your defenses and assumes you have a deal.

The add-on seems to go against a person's nature. "I got what I wanted, I better leave before he or she changes their mind."

To successfully use this tactic, stick around a while. If you are selling multiple items, sell the first one. Wait a few minutes, sell the second one. Wait a few more minutes, sell the third one, and so on. Give the buyers mind a chance to justify their decision.

This will increase your add-on sales as much as 50%.

It is like going to the grocery store and buying a chicken. I bought the chicken - I better buy the potatoes - the salad - the rolls - the dessert - and before you know it your shopping cart if full.

Contrast to make your price seem low

Nearly everyone in sales knows how to use the choice close; what day would you like delivery, Tuesday or Wednesday? What pack size would be best for you, 12 or 24? You ask the customer to choose between something you want and something else you want and them make the choice - you win both ways.

Now let's take it to a higher level by including the element of contrast. Give them a choice between something they don't want and something they didn't know they wanted until you presented the choice.

Let's say you are going to sell a house to a prospective buyer. The price you want is $200,000. You first take them to a $225,000 house that is overpriced by $25,000. Next, you take them to a $175,000 house in need of $50,000 worth of repairs located in a poor area. NOW you take

them to your perfectly priced house - $200,000. The choice for the buyer is clear.

How about the used car salesperson? They first show you an old clunker that is overpriced and barely runs. Next, they show you the car they really want to sell you. In your mind, you are comparing the differences and thinking about what a great bargain the second car is!

You are talking to a computer salesperson about purchasing a new system for your office. You tell the salesperson all your requirements who is adding everything up on your list. The salesperson now hits you with a whopping $10,000. As soon as you are over your shock you are presented with another choice - a package deal for only $3,000. What a deal! What an easy choice to make. Of course, that is what they wanted to sell you in the first place.

Consider this concept is used by Undertakers. The Undertaker will first show you a low budget, low price casket that is carefully positioned in a dark corner of the showroom. Then the deluxe model fit for a king. Then they show you the middle-priced casket and point out all the benefits.
Compared to the low-end casket and the high-end casket, it is an easy choice to make. The closing statement is usually

the one about the how the lower priced casket leaks and the higher priced doesn't!

A salesperson attending my seminar in Arizona told me about how he and his wife were prearranging their funeral. After selecting the casket out of the three choices they were offered, the Undertaker suggested that he get in and try it out. He got in and his wife said: "that's perfect, with your blue suit on you will look great!" This is the "puppy dog" close taken to an extreme!

What does this have to do with you? The next time you present a product to a customer take three products instead of one. Take in an expensive, high-end product, a low-end product, along with the one you want to sell. Show them the over-priced high-end product first, then the low- end cheap product. After they get over their shock, bring out the one you wanted to sell in the first place, and it will seem like an easy choice.

Duplicate the lottery's marketing strategy

I went to the local convenience store to buy some gas and was surprised at how busy it was. Cars were parked everywhere, however, there was no one at the gas pump. I went inside, and the line circled around the whole store.

There were about 40 people waiting in line to buy lottery tickets.   At first, I was going to leave, but the excitement was contagious, so I decided to stand in line and get a ticket even though my chance of winning was 1 in 175 million!

As I waited and talked with some of the other "winners" I was amazed at what people were willing to do to buy a ticket and how much they would spend. Why were they willing to take such a risk? Why would they spend as much as $30 to $40 dollars when the odds are so stacked against them? Wouldn't it be something if you and I could get people to buy our products and services with such enthusiasm?

There are several good marketing lessons we can take away from this experience. Lessons that can help you create your selling message that will be irresistible to your customers.

1.   Self-interest. The biggest lesson is that everyone acts out of self-interest. I call it the 98% factor. Most people spend 98% of their time thinking about themselves and 2% thinking about everything else. If your marketing is focused on trying to fit your message in the 2% of time left over your marketing will go unnoticed. What if you could get your message in the 98%-time frame like the lottery does? Is that even possible? Maybe not to the point the lottery does, but you can make a huge impact if you have the right focus. The 98% lesson is making your message about your customer, not your company.

2. People live in hope. The second lesson is that most people live in hope of a better tomorrow.

3. Brand confidence. The lottery has done an excellent job of building a brand. When you see the winners receive those huge checks you know it's the real deal. Testimonials work.

4. Reasons why. If people are given a strong "reason why" they should do something or buy something they are much more willing to take action. The reason why people buy lottery tickets is very clear and very personal; they can win a lot of money!

People spend 98% of their time thinking about themselves. To be successful, make a switch to thinking about your customers 98% of the time and you will surely have better odds of winning than 1 in 175 million.

You can sell anyone using this

How would you like to KNOW with absolute certainty that you could sell anybody? What if you had a magic key that would open the door to everyone you called on? You can! And once you know the secret formula - and apply it - your sales will take off!

You will lose all feelings of call reluctance. Your confidence will double - or even triple. Your income will increase. You will have everything you ever wanted in life.

Here it is...

Find out by careful listening and questioning what your customer wants and let them know that you are sincerely interested in helping them get it.

Too simple? Let's try it on YOU. What do you want most in life? Do you want more cash? A new home? Money in the bank? Financial security?

Now, what if someone came into your life who was sincerely interested in helping you get those things? What if they went out of their way to show you how to increase your income? What if they helped you find ways to save and invest more of the money you work so hard to make so you could become financially secure? What if they helped you find and buy the home of your dreams? Would you want to know this person a little better?

On the other hand, what if another person came into your life and all they wanted to do was sell you what THEY thought you should have? If they were overly aggressive, pushy, wanted to get you to do things you were not really interested in - how would you react?

Do you see the difference? Wouldn't it feel good to have someone who is sincerely interested in helping you succeed?

I know what you are thinking - the only person who is that interested in ME is my mother! Remember, this is not about YOU - it is about selling - it is about your customer.

Don't EXPECT anyone to be that interested in you. But that doesn't mean you cannot be that interested and helpful to your customers. This changes the whole focus.

Now I am going to show YOU how to make any amount of money you want by using this theory. You see, I AM interested in your success - I want you to sell more and make more money.

Let's say you want to make $120,000 over the next 12 months. Normally you would say to yourself - "THIS IS MY GOAL - I WILL MAKE $120,000 IN COMMISSIONS DURING THE NEXT 12 MONTHS." By taking this approach your focus is wrong.

Instead, try this... "I AM GOING TO GIVE $500 WORTH OF SERVICE EVERYDAY MONDAY THROUGH FRIDAY." Do you see the difference? Don't focus on the money - on what's in it for YOU - focus on GIVING THE SERVICE. The money will follow.

This is the New definition of selling - service. This definition is so new it is not even in the dictionary or thesaurus. The dictionary says selling means to persuade, or influence to a course of action. The thesaurus says selling is "barter, exchange, trade, traffic, and vend.

Nowhere does it say selling is SERVICE. Nowhere does it say selling is helping your customers become more successful and make more money.

Let's put it another way. How much would someone PAY YOU to listen to your sales pitch? Zero - Right? Yet people pay thousands of dollars to consultants to ask questions - find out what they want - and help them get it.

You can convey the same message to your customers. The true purpose of a consultative salesperson is to find out what your customer wants and help them get it.

To accomplish this, you must listen more than you talk. If you can get your customer to talk enough, they simply cannot disguise their real goals and real motives. They may try as hard as they can, but invariably they will "give themselves away". When they do - you have the key.

YOU KNOW WHAT THEY WANT!

Help them get it and you will have captured the true meaning of being a sales professional.

Customers don't NEED anything

Why are nearly all sales presentations focused on the wrong thing? Mainly because we are under the assumption that to sell, we have to find the needs of our customer and then work up a presentation that will demonstrate how we can help fill those needs. Here is the problem with finding needs; we are looking for something that does not really exist. No one "needs" anything. I am sure you have everything you need to get by, just as our customers do.

If you took away twenty-five percent of your competition, effective next Monday morning, how long would it take to fill the "needs" of your customers? Not long, probably a couple of weeks. It would be an exciting couple of weeks if we call on customers and asked them if they need anything and they said yes!

If we are not looking for needs, what are we looking for? Talking about what we need is not very exciting. If we stop for a moment and ask ourselves what we think about nearly every minute of the day we will find that it is the same thing everybody thinks about. Here's the answer. We think about what we want. We think about our future! To get people excited about buying from us we must go beyond the need and find out what they want. What is in their future that, with the help of our products and services, we can show them how to get it?

Every waking hour the mind of your customer glides out of the present into the future, and they see themselves as they will be tomorrow.

Politicians. Successful politicians use this concept in every speech. They know that if they want to stay in office or be elected to office, they have to know what the people want and build it into every talk they give. They never like to talk about the past and very rarely address issues in the present, it's always the future.

"I am your bridge to the 21st century".

"Your door to the future".

Travel agency. A travel agency always gives you a clear vision of where you are going, never on the trip getting there. A seven-day cruise sales presentation shows you the fun you will have on board ship, all the food and entertainment you will enjoy. However, they neglect to tell you about the 7-hour flight to Puerto Rico where you meet the ship and the 4 hours you have to stand on the dock waiting in line.

Insurance companies. The insurance industries entire existence relies on selling you the future. When you buy insurance, you spend thousands of dollars and have nothing in return except a piece of paper. They present you with a mental picture of what would happen to your family if you were to die. They show you how many people reach old age without any money or retirement. They give examples of the high cost of going to the hospital for surgery. The insurance companies are experts at getting a piece of your future. This does not mean that it is good or bad, it simply is the way they sell their products and services.

Lawyers. A good lawyer is a true artist in the area of painting future pictures. They usually do it based on fear of loss. When you tell them about your concern, they paint a picture of gloom by blowing your problem up to the maximum. Then, of course, they tell you how much work it would be to take care of it and, with no guarantees, will represent you for a fee.

Credit cards. One of the single largest goals of most people today is to have the money to pay off their credit card balances. How did so many people get in this situation where the average married couple owes around $25,000 in credit card bills. Once we look at the concept of appealing to someone's future, creating an impatience and a willingness to go in debt for things they didn't think they could live without, it is easy to understand why people borrow on their future. During the last 12 months over one million people filed personal bankruptcy to get out from under their debts.

Law enforcement. Law enforcement is similar to the way the lawyers use this powerful concept. The worst thing that could happen to an individual is to have their future taken away from them. Every time we watch a movie where someone is put behind bars with no hope, we can't help wondering how that would feel. If "would be" criminals new for a fact that they would be caught there would be no crime. What a criminal sees is getting away with something unearned. Getting caught is hardly a possibility for them.

Ninety percent of the excitement in the present is the imaginary picture we are constantly recreating in our minds of a tomorrow! To successfully present your products and services in a way that will have your customers leaning forward asking for more, talk about how you are the solution to their future problems.

Put some spice in your presentation

There is just too much ho-hum marketing going on. There are too many salespeople who just don't get the fact that enthusiasm is contagious and as a salesperson, you have to infect everyone with a good dose of excitement.

So how do you get jacked up?

Here's how to get UN-jacked. Tell yourself you are a loser.
Tell yourself you hate what you do. Tell yourself you will
never make the sale. Tell yourself your company sucks. Tell
yourself you never got any of the breaks. Tell yourself the
competition is ruthless. Tell yourself that everybody buys on
price. Tell yourself that your sales territory is saturated and
there is no business.

Do you know what ninety-five percent of everyone in prison
were told over and over again as they were growing up:
"You are going to end up in prison someday?" Think about
it. Over and over again they were told they were going to end
up in prison someday. What if they were told something
different? What if they were told over and over again that
they might be in a little trouble right now, but they will get
past it? What if they were told that they were going to grow
up and be successful? Would that make a difference? The
stuff you put in your mind is the what controls your actions.
So, to get jacked up you have to put things in your mind that
will get you excited and passionate about what you do for a
living.

Put this affirmation in your mind. Carry it around with you
and watch the difference...

(READ THIS LIKE YOU MEAN IT!) I am excited! I stay

focused on all the good things I have to be excited about. I am excited about my career, my opportunities, and my challenges. My excitement drives me to do everything with energy and enthusiasm. My mind is focused fully on what I am doing, and I can get things done by telling myself to "DO IT NOW". I am excited and act enthusiastic and everyone around me catches it. Every time I see someone I know or meet someone new I am excited and enthusiastic about seeing them. By being enthusiastic, excited and full of energy I am a more valuable person. Energy and enthusiasm guarantee my success as a highly paid professional. Energy, passion, and enthusiasm will attract customers and sales to me. This energy will be like a magnet and attract bigger customers and larger commissions to me. I am going to give everything I have to everything I do.

Don't be a daydreamer. Don't wish you were somewhere else doing something different. Life is what it is. For whatever reason, you are where you are right now, so you must deal with it. Keep this quote on your dashboard: "My job is not to see what lies dimly at a distance, but to do what lies clearly at hand!" That means there is no getting around it... you have to make the prospecting call, send the email, mail the letter, take care of the follow-up and keep going.

Forget about whether you feel like it or not. Actions come before feelings. ACT enthusiastic and your feelings will follow. If you wait until you FEEL jacked up, you will be like the woman sitting on the park bench who turned into a skeleton waiting for the perfect man. It ain't gonna happen!

Here is another way to stay excited about what you are doing. Make training a DAILY part of your schedule. Spend time EVERYDAY learning something new about your business. Get excited about bringing news and information to your customers. In other words, start selling like you mean business. There is no excuse not to! Don't think it is up to the company to train you. It is up to you. Take responsibility. Invest in yourself. Read a book, take a course, listen to a motivational speech, read your marketing product sheets.

Learn something new today. Get out there and make something happen. Call someone. Go visit a customer and bring them a new idea. Stop whining. No one said it was going to be easy! Your customers need help making good decisions. Go help them make the decision to buy from you by being excited, enthusiastic and jacked up! Let them know you really want their business!

Break free from the electronic quicksand

I just met the future CEO, President or a guy that is going to be the most amazing manager, sales manager or customer service manager you will ever know!

This guy has restored my faith in the younger generation who are accused of not being able to communicate. They are told they don't know how to interact because all they do is text each other.

No matter how long you have been in sales or management this young man has a lesson for all of us who are trying to increase the level of customer service or get our customers to buy more of our products and services.

I'm not even sure the young man realized the significance of what he did. This small act, if you became infected with, would not only turn your sales around, if everybody did it, everything could turn around.

Most of us are walking around in a daze. We've got our head buried in the sand and we don't even know what's going on around us. We are going through our day saying, "why me?" We are worried about being laid off, not being able to pay our bills, losing our customers. "Sales were going so good a few years ago, but now, everything is falling apart."

Well, this young night clerk in the La Quinta Inn demonstrated to me that if you go the extra mile with a little bit of sincere attention you can go from "why me" to "why not me?"

Here's what he did to make such an impression.

When I checked in he said: "Welcome Mr. Oros, I see you are a motivational speaker and sales trainer!"

You might be wondering what the big deal is? Here it is. My email address is Bob@BobOros.com. This young man took the initiative to look up my website to see what I do. That small, seemingly insignificant jester has NEVER been done by any of the thousands of hotels I have stayed in. None of the Hiltons, Hyatt's or Crown Plazas where I use my email address for my confirmation have ever felt that my business was important enough, or they were at least a little curious about one of their customers.

Let's compare that with my bank.

They just started a new program. When you go through the drive through, they remind you that your car payment is due!

Not: "Hello Mr. Oros, I hope you're having a great day!" All they say is: "Do you know your car payment is due?"

Here's what I was saying on the inside: "How stupid do you think I am? Of course, I know my car payment is due and it will be paid Friday, which is well within the terms of the loan!"

Why not put a little note on my account that said: "Bob Oros? Loyal customer since 1988. Over x million dollars deposited. Motivational speaker and sales trainer. Ask advice on how to get motivated.

EVERYBODY is hungry for a little attention!

What do you know about your customers? Have you been to their website? Have you read their advertisements?

It's like everybody is going around building thousands of shallow, meaningless relationships on Twitter and Facebook rather than paying attention to the person right in front of you!

When that young man looked me in the eye, welcomed me, and gave me the ultimate compliment of a little attention, he made the sale. That personal attention meant more to me than all the "tweets" on Twitter will EVER mean!

I am on an airplane on my way to do a seminar where I will be staying for three nights. Am I staying at the Hyatt? Nope. Am I staying at the Hilton? Nope. I am staying at the La Quinta to remind myself that when I meet with my customers and give my speech, to gather all the information I can, be sincerely interested in them - and pay attention!

The best advice I can give you is to get your head out of the electronic sand. Use all your "e" stuff to simplify your life. Use it as an amazing tool to collect information, communicate, learn and keep records.

But when it comes to customer service, selling, motivating your staff or building your relationships there is nothing more effective than a smile, the sound of your voice, eye contact, a handshake, a meaningful conversation, and a little sincere attention to seal the deal.

The true meaning of street smarts

It was getting dark and the traffic was heavy. I pulled off the highway to get my bearings to be sure I didn't pass the exit I was looking for. I was heading west on Interstate 20 just west of Atlanta. As soon as I pulled into a MacDonald's I learned the real meaning of being "street smart." A young man about 28 years old approached my car with a bottle of Windex in his hand. He said he needed money and he was willing to work for it. He wanted to wash my windows.

I travel a lot and I am approached by many homeless people; however, this guy seemed a little different. He had a sincere look on his face along with a slight smile that immediately removed any feelings of worry that he might be dangerous. I asked him what his name was, and he said Chad.

I told Chad it wasn't necessary to wash my windows and I bluntly asked him why an obviously talented guy like him was living on the street. He said he got out of jail three weeks ago and can't find a job. He said the standard answer everyone gives him is to come back after the first of the year. He said he has been to every place within walking distance with no luck.

I asked Chad if he had a driver's license. He said he did but couldn't get a copy of it. He said it's a catch 22. You can't get a driver's license without a birth certificate and you can't get a birth certificate without identification. I asked him where he was staying and how long it has been since he had something to eat. He sleeps during the day and tries to get enough money in the evening to get by for the day. He said he hadn't eaten yet.

I invited him into MacDonald's where we ordered dinner and sat down to eat. Chad seemed friendly and willing to talk, so I asked him some question to see if I might help point him in the right direction.

Do you have a family? "A wife and two kids, but they won't have anything to do with me."

Why were you in jail? He said he would rather not tell me. I pushed and asked him again. He said he didn't want me to be tempted to try it. I told him he didn't have to worry - I wasn't into anything illegal. He said he found a way to take the ink off of 5-dollar bills and turn them into 50's. He said everything was going well until he got caught and got sent to jail for 18 months.

Where are you from? Chad was originally from Indiana but ran away from home when he was twelve years old. He started selling drugs and by the time he was 18 he had his own home paid for and was doing well. Then he got caught and sent to jail. After he got out it was one thing after another until he came across the counterfeiting idea. That lasted a few years until he got caught again. He said he didn't have an education and could never get a job that paid more than minimum wage.

What's going to be your next scam? This was the question I was leading up to. I studied his answer carefully to see if I could sense whether he was telling the truth. He said, very sincerely, there are no more scams. If someone walked up and offered him the surest thing that could not fail, he would turn it down.

How many people help you out? He said about 2 in 10. Out of the 10, some of them are downright mean and tell me to beat it or get lost, some of them just ignore me, and some of them threaten to call the police. But I just keep going looking for that one in five. Every now and then you find someone who goes out of their way to be helpful. A lady pulled up last week and gave me two turkey dinners. I took them to some friends of mine who were on the street and not able to get money as well as I could and gave the dinners to them. On the downside, I walked up to the drive-up window to buy a sandwich because the dining room was closed, and the girl called the police.

You said you didn't have an education, but you sure got a lot of "street smarts." Chad asked me what I meant, so I asked him to tell me everything he knew about me. He said I was from out of town because my license plate said Florida, but that's not where you are from because there was a rental tag on the dashboard, so you probably flew in from somewhere. You do work with people because you were not afraid to talk to me like a lot of folks. You have 9 one-dollar bills in your wallet and about 4 twenty-dollar bills. You probably have a family and are successful at what you do.

I told Chad that is what you call genuine street smarts. I asked him how he developed the skill.

Here's what he told me:

"Being in jail and living on the street you learn these things automatically. You must be totally aware of everything that is going on around you every minute of the day. You might be in danger and have to take off, or you might miss an opportunity if you are not paying attention. After a while, it becomes a habit and it's impossible NOT to do it."

And there is our answer to what it means to be street smart. Apply that to your everyday sales and watch your business take off!!

For the next hour, I gave Chad all the help and guidance I could. I encouraged him to look for a job in direct sales. Any sales manager who would not give this guy a chance would have to have his or her head examined. Chad had more raw sales talent than anyone I have ever met.

As I was leaving, I gave Chad enough money to last a few days, buy a new set of clothes and told him to go to the truck stop, get cleaned up and head to the employment office.

Will Chad take my advice? Was I scammed? It doesn't matter. Chad taught me a great lesson, the true meaning of street smarts!

Being a consultant

"You can't describe a place you have never been."

I was driving down highway 75 in Florida and pulled off at a Long John Silver seafood restaurant for lunch. As I was entering the front door a 'panhandler' was sitting on the curb asking everyone for their spare change.

As I was eating lunch, I could see him through the window, and I thought how distracting it was to the customers. I wondered why the manager didn't ask him to leave. He had a tin can in front of him and one out of every five people dropped some change in it. I got to thinking that one out of every five is a pretty good closing ratio. One more confirmation of the 2 out of every 10 law.

After I finished eating, I walked out the door and was thinking about how I was going to avoid him. I was dressed extremely casual as my whole day consisted of simply driving from point A to point B. I have special clothes for these occasions as I don't want to travel with a whole lot of luggage. So, I have some old jeans and a special sweatshirt that my wife keeps telling me to throw away.

As we made eye contact, I made a spur-of-the- moment decision. I sat on the curb next to him. For the next 30 minutes, I learned five lessons that will stay with me for the rest of my life. Because of those 30 minutes, I am not only a better salesperson and a better speaker, I am a better person.

Lesson #1

The first lesson I learned was how it feels when someone thinks you are a bum asking for a handout. It was a strange feeling. I wanted to tell these folks who were walking by that I was not with this guy. I was just talking with him. I am not a beggar. I work for a living. Some of them looked disgusted. It was as if they were silently telling us to get a job.

One irate man said that he would give us a couple of bucks, but he rudely accused us of being a couple of drunks and the money would just be wasted.

Some people avoided eye contact with us all together. I guess they felt that if they locked eyes with either of us, they would feel an obligation to put some money in the can. After the first five minutes the concern about what people thought left me. They don't know who I am. They will never see me again. I wondered what they would think when they see me walk over to my rental car and put the top down on my convertible!

It is hard to put into words the transformation I went through after I told myself; "so what if they think I'm a bum – that's their problem, not mine!" I may have made this adjustment a lot quicker than the average person because I had sales experience I could draw on.

One of the most difficult obstacles a beginning salesperson must overcome is the concern he or she has about what people will think of them. If you are not making the calls because you are worried about what someone will think of you, here is some important insight. They are not thinking about you. They are thinking about themselves. Do you think the people who walked by me went to the restaurant and thought about me during their entire meal? The amount of time they spent thinking about me could be measured in fractions of a second. Yet, most of the reason many salespeople do not reach their full selling potential is that they are dominated by this concern about what people will think.

Lesson #2

The second lesson was that one out of every five people dropped some change in the can. I thought that was interesting. He didn't even have to say anything; the can was the presentation! The can did the job for him. He completely set the stage for the sale. He was appropriately dressed to look like a street person. There was no question about it. His old sneakers, his faded shirt, which was covered by his sleeveless sweater, his baseball hat, his unshaven face, all creating the perfect appearance of what the ideal homeless person looked like in the eyes of his "customer." And because of this carefully designed "theater" he set up, one out of five were convinced that the right thing to do was to help him (us) out. This was an interesting observation.

In my experience, if you look like a salesperson, the sale is harder to make. If you look like someone who is there to help solve a problem, you have successfully set the stage for a sale, and it comes much easier.

Try changing your image from a stereotype to a problem solver and see how much more receptive your customers will be. When you go to the gatekeeper and ask to see the manager don't introduce yourself as a salesperson. Instead, introduce yourself as a problem solver. When you are asked what this is about, answer by telling them you don't know until you ask them 3 simple questions and it takes less than three minutes.

Lesson #3

The third lesson was that he said thanks to everyone. Not just the words thank you, but a sincere - I really appreciate it - thank you. He made them feel good about putting money in his can. People like to help other people or at least one out of five do, as my research proved. Did you ever wonder what people think about after they buy something from you? They don't really expect any gratitude on the surface. But deep down inside they're screaming to be appreciated.

It is very rare for us to get the red-carpet treatment from anyone. I recently visited a store and was shocked by the excellent service. Someone met us at the door, escorted us through the aisles, answered our questions, gave us snacks to eat while we were shopping, and when we checked out, you won't believe what happened! They wrote down our name, address and birthday. Two days later we got a thank you card in the mail and a birthday card followed a few days before the big day. Now, the thing that made this so special was "we" were my dog and. It was a pet store and that's how they treated my DOG! Do you really appreciate your customers? I mean REALLY.

Lesson #4

The fourth lesson. Here is his story. His name is Ralph and he lived in South Carolina. He lost his job and on the very same day, his wife left him. She cleaned out their apartment, their bank accounts and maxed all the credit cards by taking cash advances. He was left with the clothes he had in the apartment closet and about $20 in his pocket. He had no family, so he packed a small suitcase and went to the local truck stop where he hitched a ride to Florida. He had been there a month when I ran into him. I asked him all the questions you would ask. Have you looked for a job? "I can't even get a job as a day laborer without a Florida address. I have no transportation, no place to live, no friends, no credit and no money. All I can do is find someplace to set up for the day and see if enough folks will help me, so I can buy a meal." He spends every night trying to find a place to unroll his sleeping bag.

The lesson that Ralph taught me was this: I have absolutely nothing to complain about. Nothing! I stood up to leave, opened my wallet and gave Ralph fifty dollars. That was by far the best sales, marketing, and motivation training I have ever received in my entire life.

Lesson #5

The fifth lesson. Even though I talked with Ralph for 30 minutes, and for a moment knew the feeling of what it was like to be perceived as a street person, I couldn't begin to describe what it must be like to live on the street.

Why?

Because it is impossible to describe a place you have never been. Before someone assumes the role of teacher or trainer they have to know – really know – what they are talking about. They cannot spend 30 minutes next to a client or customer on a curb asking questions and think they know what it is like to have the problems they are dealing with.

You see, a consultant really must KNOW. Let me give you an example of KNOWING.

The manager of a school cafeteria must KNOW this. Let's say the holidays are approaching and the manager is going to cook turkeys for the school kids. The turkeys are stuffed the night before and put in the refrigerator overnight. The result: putting warm stuffing in a cold turkey overnight will cause botulism spores to grow which will create a toxin that cannot be killed by cooking. If there are onions in the stuffing, they will accelerate the growth of the spores. The turkeys are cooked the next day and the school kids get sick. If they are not rushed to the hospital the toxin will cause the children to die of botulism poisoning.

Anything less than this type of KNOWING is the same as trying to tell someone how it feels to live on the street based on a chance conversation with a person who IS living on the street.

Do you know what you are talking about? I mean really KNOW. That is the foundation for being extremely successful in your selling and negotiating efforts.

10 best copywriting formulas

A great idea is to copy and paste these to different color notes and glue them to a poster board. When you are stuck on what to write, or where to start, study the board and pick a formula.

1. Before – After – Bridge

Before – Here's your world …
After – Imagine what it'd be like
Bridge – Here's how to get there.

2. Problem – Agitate – Solve

Identify a problem
Agitate the problem
Solve the problem

3. Features – Advantages – Benefits (FAB)

Features – What you or your product can do
Advantages – Why this is helpful
Benefits – What it means for the person reading

4. The 4 U's

Useful – Be useful to the reader

Urgent – Provide a sense of urgency

Unique – Convey a benefit that is unique

Ultra-specific – Be ultra-specific with all of the above

5. Attention Interest Desire Action (AIDA)

Attention – Get the reader's attention

Interest –Information that appeals to the reader

Desire – Benefits of your product/service/idea

Action – Ask for a response

6. The 5 basic objections

1. I don't have enough time.
2. I don't have enough money.
3. It won't work for me
4. I don't believe you.
5. I don't need it.

7. Write to one person

Good advertising is written from one person to another.

8. The 3 Reasons Why

Why are you the best?

Why should I believe you?

Why should I buy right now?

9. So what?

Every time you state something, ask yourself, "So what?"

10. The Fan Dancer

Be specific without actually explaining anything. The Fan Dancer formula uses specific details to create curiosity, never revealing any actual information about what that tantalizing something is. To find out, someone will need to click or keep reading.

About the author

Regardless of whether you are reading one of his books or attending one of his presentations, the most frequent comment is: "This guy has been there, he is one of us, I am going to use these strategies." With over 2,000 presentations in all 50 states and as far away as New Zealand, as well as being a CSP (Certified Speaking Professional, the highest designation awarded by the National Speakers Association and the International Federation for Professional Speakers), you can feel confident you will get the results you are looking for.

www.ingramcontent.com/pod-product-compliance
Lightning Source LLC
Chambersburg PA
CBHW030008190526
45157CB00014B/1091